PHIL DAVIES

Firebird is Phil's debut full-length play.

Phil trained at the Royal Court Young Writers Programme where he developed his first script, *Adjusted*, which won the Rod Hall Memorial Award and gained him an attachment with Paines Plough.

Other work includes short play *How To Not Murder* (Arcola Theatre, dir. Ned Bennett); *Up the Dale* (Royal Exchange Theatre and Queen Elizabeth Hall for Paines Plough); *Adjusted* (Interplay Europe, Utrecht) and *The Makings* (ATG, dir. Sarah Dickinson). Earlier this year, Phil was commissioned by LAMDA to write a short film for their 2015 graduates programme – consequently *Face* was screened at Curzon Soho Cinema.

Most recently Phil has been working alongside Synergy Theatre Project developing scripts with inmates at Feltham Young Offenders Institution, as well as teaching in a secondary school in South East London.

Other Titles in this Series

Mike Bartlett
BULL
GAME
AN INTERVENTION
KING CHARLES III

Tom Basden
THE CROCODILE
HOLES
JOSEPH K
THERE IS A WAR

Deborah Bruce
THE DISTANCE
GODCHILD
SAME

Jez Butterworth
JERUSALEM
JEZ BUTTERWORTH PLAYS: ONE
MOJO
THE NIGHT HERON
PARLOUR SONG
THE RIVER
THE WINTERLING

Caryl Churchill
BLUE HEART
CHURCHILL PLAYS: THREE
CHURCHILL PLAYS: FOUR
CHURCHILL: SHORTS
CLOUD NINE
DING DONG THE WICKED
A DREAM PLAY *after* Strindberg
DRUNK ENOUGH TO SAY
    I LOVE YOU?
FAR AWAY
HOTEL
ICECREAM
LIGHT SHINING IN
    BUCKINGHAMSHIRE
LOVE AND INFORMATION
MAD FOREST
A NUMBER
SEVEN JEWISH CHILDREN
THE SKRIKER
THIS IS A CHAIR
THYESTES *after* Seneca
TRAPS

Vivienne Franzmann
MOGADISHU
PESTS
THE WITNESS

James Fritz
ROSS & RACHEL

debbie tucker green
BORN BAD
DIRTY BUTTERFLY
HANG
NUT
RANDOM
STONING MARY
TRADE & GENERATIONS
TRUTH AND RECONCILIATION

Vicky Jones
THE ONE

Anna Jordan
CHICKEN SHOP
FREAK
YEN

Lucy Kirkwood
BEAUTY AND THE BEAST
    with Katie Mitchell
BLOODY WIMMIN
CHIMERICA
HEDDA *after* Ibsen
IT FELT EMPTY WHEN THE
    HEART WENT AT FIRST BUT
    IT IS ALRIGHT NOW
NSFW
TINDERBOX

Laura Lomas
BIRD & OTHER MONOLOGUES FOR
    YOUNG WOMEN

Cordelia Lynn
LELA & CO.

Chloë Moss
CHRISTMAS IS MILES AWAY
HOW LOVE IS SPELT
FATAL LIGHT
THE GATEKEEPER
THE WAY HOME
THIS WIDE NIGHT

Evan Placey
CONSENSUAL
GIRLS LIKE THAT
GIRLS LIKE THAT & OTHER PLAYS
    FOR TEENAGERS
PRONOUN

Stef Smith
REMOTE
SWALLOW

Jack Thorne
2ND MAY 1997
BUNNY
BURYING YOUR BROTHER IN
    THE PAVEMENT
HOPE
JACK THORNE PLAYS: ONE
LET THE RIGHT ONE IN
    after John Ajvide Lindqvist
MYDIDAE
STACY & FANNY AND FAGGOT
THE SOLID LIFE OF SUGAR WATER
WHEN YOU CURE ME

Phoebe Waller-Bridge
FLEABAG

Tom Wells
JUMPERS FOR GOALPOSTS
THE KITCHEN SINK
ME, AS A PENGUIN

Phil Davies

FIREBIRD

NICK HERN BOOKS

London

www.nickhernbooks.co.uk

A Nick Hern Book

Firebird first published in Great Britain as a paperback original in 2015 by Nick Hern Books Limited, The Glasshouse, 49a Goldhawk Road, London W12 8QP

Firebird copyright © 2015 Phil Davies

Phil Davies has asserted his right to be identified as the author of this work

Cover image: www.istockphoto.com/Kativ

Designed and typeset by Nick Hern Books, London

Printed in the UK by CPI Group (UK) Ltd

A CIP catalogue record for this book is available from the British Library

ISBN 978 1 84842 530 9

Firebird was first performed at Hampstead Theatre Downstairs, London, on 24 September 2015. The cast was as follows:

TIA	Callie Cooke
KATIE	Tahirah Sharif
AJ/SIMON	Phaldut Sharma

Director	Edward Hall
Designer	Polly Sullivan
Lighting	Tom Nickson
Sound	John Leonard

Acknowledgements

I am indebted to many people for the production of this play:

Ed Hall for everything, not least performing the unenviable task of getting inside my head with such sharpness, passion and diligence.

Will Mortimer for meeting Agent Kel and kicking it all off.

Callie, Tahira and Phaldut for their electricity and commitment and for not saving me any cake.

Polly for putting Rochdale in a box. Sophia for holding it all together.

Aron Rollin, Tim Sanders and Jude Williams for their generosity during the research for this play.

Russ Davies, Celia De Wolff, Katie Langridge and Tanya Tillett for reading and supporting and suggesting.

Thanks to all at NHB for being so meticulous and so lovely.

Above all, I wish to acknowledge all the Firebirds who have been and – unacceptably – those who will be. May the play's subject matter soon be obsolete.

P.D.

For Kellie Shirley, who pushed and pushed and pushed

Characters

TIA, *fourteen to fifteen*
KATIE, *fourteen*
AJ, *late twenties/early thirties*
SIMON, *thirties*

AJ and Simon to be played by the same actor.

The play takes place in Greater Manchester and spans approximately nine months.

Punctuation

A forward slash (/) indicates the point at which speech overlaps

A dash (–) indicates an interruption to speech or train of thought

An ellipsis (…) indicates an inability to articulate or a trailing off

This text went to press before the end of rehearsals and so may differ slightly from the play as performed.

1.

October, 2014.

A bridge over a small river on the edge of town. Bright sunshine.

KATIE *pushes and spins* TIA *around in a wheelchair. One of* TIA*'s legs is almost entirely covered in plaster.* TIA *is clutching an open bottle of champagne.*

KATIE. I love it here!

TIA. Told yer.

KATIE. So pretty.

    TIA *hands the bottle to* KATIE.

TIA. See?

KATIE. You can see for miles and miles and miles.

TIA. Beats havin to look at flaky Bennett.

KATIE. I didn't even know you had countryside.

TIA. Bet London's nicer.

KATIE. Don't get this in London. Look at all the hills and the fields and all those tiny houses dotted about on their own. Imagine living in one of them. I'd love that. Just me and Mum and a big log fire and –

TIA. Fuck knows how yer gunna get me back up there.

KATIE. Oh Tia, I love it here!

TIA. Calm down, it's only a few fields.

KATIE. I'm so glad you came Centre!

TIA. Think someone's gettin a bit tipsy.

KATIE. I think they are!

KATIE *passes* TIA *the bottle*.

Let's play a game.
Can we?
A game I used to really like
And I mean *really* like –
Oh my god you're gonna love it –
It's that game where you pretend you're on like another planet and –

TIA. Don't know it.

KATIE. Yeah anyway I'll explain. It's like you're on another planet that's actually really similar to this planet but it's different in like different ways and –
Do you know which game I mean?

TIA. No.

KATIE. Tryna think of the name.
Anyway it's easy. You'll get it. I'm just
I'll explain it better.

TIA. Have some.

KATIE. Hold on. Let me explain the rules.

TIA. Have some first.

KATIE. Did you even have any? You didn't even have any.

TIA. I had a massive swig, what yer on about?

KATIE. I didn't notice.

    KATIE *takes the bottle and drinks*.

TIA. More than that.

KATIE. Wait.

TIA. Don't be a pussy.

KATIE. I'm not.

    KATIE *drinks some more. She burps and they both laugh.*

    Champagne's proper mingin.

TIA. Innit.

KATIE. Posh people bare love it though.

TIA. Shoulda got White Star.

KATIE. Posh people got no taste.

TIA. Probably woulda got two two-litre bottles of White Star.
Easy.

KATIE. Four litres of White Star?

TIA (*indicating wheelchair*). Yer can hide shitloads in here and
no one suspects yer.

KATIE. So the rules right…

TIA. Don't wanna play a game.

KATIE. Oh come on it's fun you'll love it –

TIA. Do a look like a can play a game?

KATIE. Ah but you don't have to move so even people in
wheelchairs can play so –
Feelin proper pissed!

TIA. And we still got the vodka. I'm gunna drink so much that I
don't know which way up the sky is. An the best thing is I
can't fall over.

KATIE. Okay. The rules. You gotta imagine there's this other
planet that's just like this one –

TIA. Don't wanna imagine that I'm on another planet or owt
else to do with yer crap game. Actin like some kind of kid,
Katie.

KATIE. No I'm not –
Anyway, I am one –
And so are you –
So what's wrong with acting like a kid if I am one?

TIA. Yeah but not a six-year-old
You're acting like a six-year-old.

KATIE. No I'm not. Six-year-olds wouldn't be able to play this.
They wouldn't understand it. This game's for teenagers. Bet
ya there's millions of teenagers round the world playing this
game right now.

TIA. Bet yer there's not.

KATIE. Come on. Just try it and if you don't like it we'll stop
and then we can do whatever you want.

TIA. What*ever* I want?

KATIE. Yeah.

TIA. And you'll do it?

KATIE. Yeah.

TIA. Bring it on. Let's go.

KATIE. Right, so imagine you're on a planet just like this one
Except
Except
I'm not explaining this very well.

TIA. Yer damn right.

KATIE. Basically you get the chance to imagine that you're
whoever you want to be and your life is like however you
want it to be and the world is still kind of the same except the
difference is, is that you're somebody else. Well not exactly
somebody else because you're still you but different because
you're able to have your life exactly how you want it
You get me?

TIA. …

KATIE. So one person imagines their life being exactly how it
would be in a perfect world –
That's what it's called. My Perfect World.
Honestly, you never played it?

TIA. Admit it, you've just made it up.

KATIE. I ain't I swear!
Right, watch. I'm gonna be me but on a different planet
On a different planet but similar
And I'm gonna be me but not. Right?

TIA. …

KATIE. And I'm gonna act like I would if I was on that planet
and you've gotta work out what I've changed.
Okay?

TIA. If I say yes will that get it over and done with quicker?

KATIE. Tia, come on. Give it a –

TIA. Okay yes! I'll do it. I've gotta guess… –

KATIE. What I've changed about my life.
Ready?

KATIE takes out her mobile phone and pretends she's making a call. She struts up and down.

(*Attempting an American accent.*) Hello? Yes. Hi!
It's Katie and I
Yes
We need another six lionesses and four lions
Yes. That would be nice.
And get me as many giraffes as you can. We got plenty of room here
Some Indian elephants, some African elephants
Bengal tigers and –
(*Breaking off.*) You've got to guess. Guess what I've changed.
(*Into phone again.*) And… Oh. My. God
DO NOT forget the baby sloths!
Aren't they just a*dor*able
And did you know they make great pets too – they only go to the bathroom once a week!
I know!
We're gonna need to get some feed for all these guys so make sure you get that and
(*Breaking off.*) Come on, guess! What have I changed? What am I being?

TIA.…

KATIE. Come on! Say some guesses! What job have I got?

TIA. Yer off yer head you.

KATIE. What have I changed about my life?

TIA. I don't know.

KATIE. What am I doing?

TIA. Being a massive dick?

KATIE. Come on, play!

TIA. I don't know what you want me to do. You're mincing around, chattin shit about all these different animals and I have no –

KATIE. So if I'm talking about animals…
What do you think I'm being? What job do you think I've got?

TIA. I don't know!

KATIE. What jobs are to do with animals?

TIA. How'm I meant to know?

KATIE. Have a guess!

TIA. Pet shop?

KATIE. No! Don't be stupid! I couldn't fit all of them in a pet shop!

TIA turns her wheelchair away from KATIE.

TIA. Fuck this.

KATIE. Have another guess.

TIA. Not playin.

KATIE. Why not?

TIA. Shit game.

KATIE. Please. You were getting close.

TIA. Don't care. Not doin it no more.

Pause.

KATIE. You were doing well, for your first time.
You were close an that. To getting it.

Shall we, erm
If you want we could
If
You did well Tia. Almost got it.

I think that if you had one more guess, you'd –

TIA. Don't want one more guess!

KATIE. Right
    Okay.

Pause.

    Shall I tell you?
    Do you want me to tell you the answer?

TIA. Do what you want.

KATIE. Only if you want me to.

TIA. I don't care.

KATIE. Okay.
    I'll just…
    Just so that you know…
    What I was being –
    What I'd *changed* was
    Was that I owned the biggest zoo in the world and I was able
    to look after as many animals as I wanted.
    And…

    See? You were close. The owner of a pet shop and the owner
    of a zoo are like really similar
    Well done Tia. You did so well for your first time.

    Sorry.

Pause.

TIA. Let me tell you something Katie, right. You wanna know
    why yer've never had nobody interested in yer? Yer wanna
    know why yer've never had a boyfriend? Do you / wanna
    know?

KATIE. But I have had a boyfriend.

TIA. It's because you go round acting like that, like a stupid /
    little girl.

KATIE. But I have had a boyfriend.

TIA. So immature.

KATIE. But I have had a boyfriend.

TIA. Sure.

KATIE. In London.

TIA. Sure.

KATIE. Sanchez.

TIA. *Sanchez?*

KATIE. Went out for ages.

TIA. How long?

KATIE. Three months nearly.

TIA. I've thought of a game. And you said I could choose any
game I wanted so you can't say no. It's called You Never.
Heard of it?

KATIE *shakes her head.*

What yer gotta do, right, is guess things that the other person
an't never done, like I'd say some't like
You never been to America or
You never had a period
And if I'm right, you gotta have a swig
And if I'm wrong, you gotta tell me all about it to prove
it's true.
And you can't lie. You've gotta swear on your mum's life
before we start that you'll tell the truth, the whole truth and
nowt but the truth.
Right?

KATIE *nods.*

I swear on me mum's life that I'll tell the truth, the whole
truth and nowt but the truth.
You say it now.

KATIE. I like My Perfect World better.

TIA. You promised I could play whatever I wanted. Now say it.
I swear…

KATIE. I swear on my mum's life that I'll tell the truth, the
whole truth and nothin but the truth.

TIA. I'll go first. You never met no one famous.

KATIE.…

TIA. Well have yer or not?

KATIE. I'm not sure but when I was in Year 4 this guy who
wrote a book about a horse in the war or something came to
our school and we all got to sit on his knee and –

TIA. That dun't count. He's not famous. Drink.

KATIE *drinks*.

Gotta have more than that.

KATIE *drinks*.

Your go.

KATIE. You never…
Ridden a horse

TIA. That's true. I an't.

TIA *drinks*.

Girl at my old school said riding an horse broke her in
Slag
You never… Kissed anyone
An I'm talking about proper kissed. Not pecking.

KATIE. I have.

TIA. Who, *Sanchez*?

KATIE *nods*.

Tell me then. Yer've swore on yer mother's life remember.

KATIE. We was on the park that you have to walk across to get
to school, at my old school. And there was me and Sanchez
and Megan Baxter and Theo and they started kissing and we
had to so we did.
My turn. You never fell down stairs when you did that to
your leg.

TIA. Why you asking that?

KATIE. Answer me.

TIA. Course I did.

KATIE. You've swore on your mum's life. Remember?

TIA. Yeah.

KATIE. So you can't lie.

TIA. I do know. It was me who taught you the rules.

KATIE. You never fell down stairs when you did that.

Short pause.

TIA. Gutted for yer, cos I did. Outside the flat there's concrete steps leading down to the ground floor. I fell down em when I were off me face. That's the truth.

KATIE. Swear on your mum's life.

TIA. I swear on my mum's life.

Pause.

You never been fingered.

KATIE. Tia!

TIA. What?

KATIE. Disgusting!

TIA. What?

KATIE. Can't ask me that!

TIA. Why not?

KATIE. Disgusting!

TIA. That's a no then. Drink.

KATIE. Who says it's a no?

TIA. I can tell.

KATIE. No you can't.

TIA. Can. You an't never done owt with a guy.

KATIE. Who says?

TIA. It's obvious.

KATIE. You don't know.

TIA. Remember: you can't lie. Yer've swore on yer mother's life. You never been fingered.

Pause.

See. Drink.

KATIE. Does it count if…

TIA. What?

KATIE. Never mind.

TIA. Go on.

KATIE. Does it count if it was like…
Not properly inside but
Through my leggings?

TIA *bursts out laughing.*

TIA. What, if it were through yer clothes? Course it dun't count!

TIA, *still laughing, holds the bottle out to* KATIE.

You're such a virgin!

KATIE. Don't laugh at me.

TIA. Drink!

KATIE. Stop laughing at me.

TIA. But you thought you could get fingered through your clothes!

KATIE. Please stop laughing at me.

TIA. Funny fucker!

KATIE. Stop laughing at me.

TIA. I can't help it.

KATIE. Right it's my turn now
My turn. You never –

TIA. Does it count if it's through your leggings!

TIA *bursts out laughing again.*

KATIE (*roars*). It's my go.

> *Silence.*

> KATIE *takes a swig from the bottle. And another. And another.*

> You've never had any friends.

TIA. What?

KATIE. You heard.

TIA. Course I have.

KATIE. Not proper ones.

TIA. Yes I have.

KATIE. Who?

> *Short pause.*

TIA. Loads.

KATIE. You ain't ever mentioned anyone. Not one.

TIA. So?

KATIE. Who then?

> *Short pause.*

TIA. Are you not?

> *A beat.*

KATIE. I meant apart from me.

TIA. But you didn't say that so it dun't count. My turn.
  You never had sex.

KATIE. Tia, why are you –

TIA. You said we could play anything I wanted.

KATIE. I don't want to play no more.

TIA. This'll be the last turn.
  You never had sex.

KATIE. Why do you even want to know?

TIA. Come on. What's the matter?
Even if you haven't, what's wrong with that? It's fine. We're just getting to know each other better. That's what we're doing.
So...
You never had sex

Pause.

KATIE *drinks from the bottle.*

I knew it! I knew it from day one!
From day one I knew you were a virgin
(*Sings.*) Katie is a virgin, a virgin, a virgin
Katie's never done it, done it, done it
Like a virgin! Whoo! Touched for the very first time.

I knew it!

TIA *laughs and gives herself a round of applause.*

KATIE. Please stop.

TIA. I'm like a detective. I could see it a mile off
I'm so good.

KATIE. Stop laughing at me.

TIA. It's official: Cockney Katie's never / had her –

KATIE. I don't know why you're being such a bitch but you can fuck off if you think I'm going to stay here and be laughed at.

KATIE *upends* TIA*'s wheelchair, causing her to fall to the floor.* KATIE *then pours champagne on* TIA *and drops the bottle as she exits.*

TIA. Watch what yer doin!
Yer've soaked me!
Oi! Katie! Where yer going?
Oi!
Come back!
I can't get up there on my own can I!
Katie!

TIA *tries to drag herself towards the bottle of champagne but the pain is too much for her. Her phone rings. She looks at the phone, leaves it ringing. She curls up on the floor.*

Blackout.

2.

January, 2014.

A kebab shop.

AJ *sat at a table eating.*

TIA *bursts in, drenched from rain. Staggers up to the counter.*

TIA. Chucking it down out there, dogs drownin and everythin! Can you do me a favour? I'm freezing an I really need chips. Look at me. Just some chips. I got money.

TIA *slams some pennies onto the counter and counts it.*
See. There's nearly fourteen pee there. Come on mate. (*Beat.*) Pleeeeease. Gimme chips. And one of them – whatever that is – one of them browny-yellow things. I'll pay you back – promise.
Not drunk. I'm not. I can prove it. I can walk in a straight line, watch...

TIA *walks along an imaginary line, almost straight.*

See? An I can do an handstand. Wanna see? Will yer give us chips if I do an handstand? Watch me...

After a few failed attempts, TIA *manages to perform a handstand. There's a bit of a wobble and then she collapses in a heap.*

I'm alright. I'm alright.

TIA *gets to her feet and returns to the counter.*

You gotta admit that were good –
Oi! Where yer goin?

I thought you said I could have some if I did an handstand?
Aw come on mate, look at it out there an I an't even got a
coat. Do you not care if I catch hyper-fuckin-whatsit?
Call me a skank?
I heard yer. You called me a skank.
I swear, yer gettin me angry now
I an't got no more money or I'd pay wun't I you stupid
Paki bastard!

AJ *stands*.

AJ. Whoa whoa whoa, easy tiger.

TIA. Don't talk to me.

AJ. Easy. Just seeing if I can help.

TIA. You don't know how to help. None of you lot do.

AJ. You wanna be careful. Soundin a bit racist.

TIA. Callin me a racist? Who are you to call me a racist?

AJ. I didn't actually say –

TIA. I an't got a racist bone in ma body. You're the racists,
callin me white this an white that all't time. Pervs.

AJ. Are you saying every Asian man is a perv?

TIA. Not every *Asian* man. Every *man*. See? Equality. So shut
up. (*Pause*.) What yer looking at?

AJ. That's what I'm trying to work out.

TIA. You can sit back down now.

AJ. That's very kind of you, Your Majesty. I was going to sit
down anyway.

AJ *sits down and resumes eating*.

TIA. As if yer gunna go out of business just cos of a portion of
chips. Yer proper tight you. Hey listen. Mate. Listen. Do you
a deal. Gimme chips now, yeah, and I'll put it on Twitter that
this is the best kebab shop in Rochdale. I've got four
hundred and ninety-six followers, know a lot of people,
bring you loads of business.

AJ. You really want them chips don't you.

TIA. What's it to you? Sayin I'm fat?

AJ. No, no way. I'm not saying anything like that. There's nothing of you.

TIA. Oi! Is someone gonna serve me or what?

AJ. Yo Mushy. Come out here and sort this girl some chips.

TIA. Yeah come on Mushy. My little Mushy Pea. Let me have some chips.

TIA's *phone rings*.

(*Answering phone*.) Where a yer? What d'yer mean, where am I? As if I'm still gunna be waitin there.

AJ (*standing up*). Yo Mushy!

AJ *goes behind the counter and into the back*.

TIA (*into phone*). Well I'm not there now am a! What am a gunna do, sit there like a –
Sit there like some –
No!
You said –
No, you said you'd –
Don't care. You'd better come find me
Kebab shop.
That's what it's called: *The Kebab Shop*
Ask someone
Top of town. Where the council building is.
Yeah.
Yeah, near't police station
Hurry up. How long will yer be?
Why'd yer think? I'm wet through. I'm freezin. Got no money…
So hurry up then!
Why'd you always have to do what he says? His bum-boy aren't yer. Why can't yer –
Is it? Is that it? If that's what yer think of me you know what you can do then don't yer?

TIA *cancels the call and puts the phone away*.

(*Shaking her head.*) What a… –
Tell yer what it is, right… I tell yer what it is…

AJ *returns with a carton of chips.*

AJ. What is it?

TIA. People… Let-downs the lot of em.

AJ. Hopefully these'll cheer you up.

TIA. They mine? Praise the Lord baby Jesus, Allah and all't other gods – I've got ma chips!

AJ. Why don't you sit down? Rest your legs.

TIA. I was gunna sit down anyway.

AJ. Does Mademoiselle require any ketchup or anything?

TIA *opens the cardboard tray and starts eating the chips.*

TIA. Salt.

AJ. I put some on.

TIA. More.

AJ. I put quite a bit on –

TIA. More salt.

AJ *walks to the counter.*

And some cheese.

AJ. Cheese? On chips?

TIA. That's what I said. Cheese.

AJ. Gotta tell ya, that sounds proper dark.

TIA. See if they've got some, there's a good boy.

AJ. Get a load of this one.

AJ *goes behind the counter and disappears into the back.*

TIA. These are the best chips! I love you Mushy Pea!

AJ *returns with a salt shaker, a bottle of Coke and some small items wrapped in paper. He places them on the table.*

TIA *grabs the salt shaker and shakes salt over the chips.*

AJ. That's a crazy amount of salt.

TIA. 'S how I like it. Salty.

> AJ *reveals a cheese slice in a packet.* TIA *looks at the cheese and laughs.*

> What the hell's that?

AJ. You said cheese.

TIA. How'm I meant to put that on ma chips?

AJ. Just... I dunno. Put it on.

> TIA *inspects the cheese slice.*

TIA (*laughing*). What am I meant to do with this?

AJ. Mind if I sit down?

TIA. Do what you want. (*Struggling to unwrap the cheese slice.*) How'd yer get this wrapper open – ?

AJ. Pass it here.

> AJ *reaches for the cheese slice but* TIA *moves it away.*

TIA. Don't touch it.

AJ. Why? (*Beat.*) Don't want my dirty brown hands to give you any diseases?

TIA. That's not it, I just –

> TIA *looks like she might throw up.*

AJ. Are you alright?

> TIA *takes a swig of the Coke.*

> TIA *burps.*

TIA. Oh that's better. Flipping heck, I needed that.

AJ. Wow.

TIA. Thought I were gunna spew.

AJ. I can see. I'm AJ.

TIA. Oh right.

AJ. What about you? What's your name?

TIA. Not tellin yer.

AJ. Why not?

TIA. Why'd yer need to know for?

AJ. I think knowing someone's name helps you understand what they're like.

TIA. I don't.

AJ. Some people say that what you're called has like an effect on who you are, on your personality and that. Look at him – don't he look like a Mushy? Or... I dunno... don't Beyoncé proper look like a Beyoncé? She don't look like no Mildred –

TIA. That's cos she *is* Beyoncé? Am tryna eat anyway so...

AJ. Imagine if she was though – Mildred! Not the same. Imagine if I was called, I don't know... Imagine if I was called –

TIA. Imagine if you was called – (*Puts finger to her lips.*) Shhhhhhh

AJ. So rude. Okay, imagine if I was called Shhhhhh –

TIA. Shhhhh.

AJ. It's actually interesting –

TIA. Shhhhh.

AJ. Okay. I'll shut up if you tell me your name.

TIA. Donna.

AJ. Donna?

TIA. Yep.

AJ. For real?

TIA. Yep. Donna kebab.

TIA *laughs*.

AJ. What's your real name? Come on. What should I call you?

TIA. Whatever. I don't care.

AJ. I can call you what I want?

TIA. As long as it shuts you up.

AJ. Alright. I'll call you… Honey. Because you're sweet. What do you think of that?

TIA. Cringe. My name's Tia. (*Beat.*) What's in there? Looks proper greasy.

AJ. Those browny-yellow things you're interested in happen to be the finest onion bhajis this side of Lahore.

TIA. Onion what?

AJ. Onion bhajis. Don't tell me you've never heard of onion bhajis.

TIA. They look rank.

AJ. Try it.

TIA. No chance.

AJ. Don't be afraid of new things.

TIA. I'm not. Spontaneous me.

AJ (*eating a bhaji*). That is so good. You're supposed to have a dip with it and then it's even better but, boy, they're still delicious. Go on, try.

TIA. You're alright.

AJ. Suit yourself.

TIA. Was Honey the best name you could come up with?

AJ. I like it. Suits you.

TIA. It dun't. Should've called me Dog.

AJ. What you on about –

TIA. Should've called me Pig.

AJ. Why you saying that?

TIA. You know Honey dun't suit me. Face it.

AJ. It does! Honey is sweet. And so are you.

TIA. Shut up.

AJ. It's true.

TIA. I'm horrible.

AJ. Why you saying that?

TIA. Because I know.

AJ. It's not true. And if there are people who tell you that, they're wrong. I hope you don't believe it.

TIA. You sound like a social worker.

AJ. And what does a social worker sound like?

TIA. Like you. 'Oh, I can sense you've got a lot of negative feelings coming from you. Maybe you should try to feel more positive and then you'll be able to blah-dee-blah all I eat is salad even though I'm fat and think I can go round tellin people how to live.' Like that.

AJ. I didn't know I sounded like that. It's probably because of my job.

Short pause.

AJ *laughs.*

TIA. What's so funny?

AJ. I thought that you might at least –

TIA. Ask you what yer job is?

AJ. Yes. That's what people do when –

TIA. I knew you wanted me to ask. But I don't play that game. I find it well annoying if I'm honest. Girls at school do it all't time. You're like one o' t'girls at school.

AJ. Is that right? No one's ever told me that before.

TIA. They say some't or sigh or start laughing and then wait for you to ask em why. Drives me mad. 'It's probably because of my job.'

AJ. I can sense you've got a lot of negative feelings coming from you –

TIA. Do one.

AJ. You're funny you know. You're a joker.
Anyway, if you're not going to ask I'll tell you. I'm a youth worker.

TIA. Good for you.

AJ. Thought you might like to know.

TIA. Well you're wrong. (*Beat*.) You can leave me alone now.

AJ. Now you've got your free chips? Seems a bit rude.

TIA. Told yer. Not a nice person.

AJ *receives a text message.*

AJ. Sorry. Just need to…

AJ *responds to the text and then places the phone on the table.*

I've gotta tell you, if one of the kids I'm looking after was out this late on a school night, I'd be proper worried about them.

TIA. School night.

AJ. That's what it is.

TIA. Makes me sound like I'm a six-year-old.

AJ. So who's going to be worrying about you?

TIA. I'm allowed out this late.

AJ. Who says?

TIA. I say.

AJ. So you decide what time you have to be home?

TIA. Yep.

AJ. And your mum and dad don't say anything?

TIA. I can do what a want.

AJ. I just would've thought that –

TIA. How much do you get paid being a youth worker?

AJ. Not that much.

TIA. How comes you got a nice suit then? How comes you look all smart?

AJ. Off to a party later. Anyway, you know what they say, dress for the job you want not the job you've got.

TIA. What job do you want?

AJ. I'm happy with my job, to be honest.

TIA. So why'd you say that about dressing for the job you want then?

AJ. I don't know, I guess I was just. It's just a figure of / speech I guess.

TIA. You're a liar. That's why.

AJ. You what?

TIA. You're not a youth worker. I can see right through you.

AJ. What you on about?

TIA. I know what you are.

AJ. I honestly have no idea what you're –

TIA. You're the fucking…
    You're the secret millionaire!

    AJ *laughs*.

    You are. I can tell it a mile off
    Get yer chequebook out! Buy me a flat!

AJ. Joker. I'm really not.

TIA. You don't fool me. I always knew I'd suss it out. I said it. If they ever came here, I'd know. Where are't cameras? You've probably got one of those pinhole cameras in your suit an't yer.

AJ. I haven't. I'm not the –

TIA. Or they're hiding outside. Are they outside? Where are they? Let me find em.

AJ. There's no point looking out there. There are no cameras.

TIA. I said to ma nan that I'd be able to spot one. I said it.
And she said everyone always knows but the trick is not
to make it...
Obvious...
Oh...
Can we just pretend I don't know? You can delete that bit
when I found out can't yer. Let's pretend it din't happen.

AJ. You're funny, man! I'm not the secret millionaire. I wish I
was. Come on, sit back down. There are no cameras.

TIA. Are we pretending now?

AJ. No, I'm telling you. I'm not a millionaire!

TIA. I'm a well good actress. You'd better write me a cheque at
the end. What's so funny?

AJ. My name's AJ and I'm a youth worker.

TIA. Oh, right. Are we...?
(*Acting as if on the programme.*) A youth worker? That's
well good. What does a youth worker do?

AJ. I told you.

TIA. That's so nice of you. That's a well good job. A youth
worker. You're probably looking for some youths to work
with. I might be able to help. I live on the Freehold Estate.
And if you knew Freehold, you'd know it's a proper / dive.

AJ. I do know Freehold. I am from –

TIA. A proper black hole. I know everyone thinks they're from
rough places an that. Think they're from bad areas. But
Freehold dun't mess about. I mean, it's top of t'country when
it comes to being crap. Won awards for it. Saw it on't news.
Best amount of unemployment or some't –

AJ. Stop, I do know –

TIA. It's true. Nobody's got a job, nobody's got money,
nobody's got owt. And if you do have owt it gets nicked by
all't smackheads and thieves. You should come and see it.
I'll look after yer. Come on, come down and have a look.

See all't dogshit and broken glass and all't dead-eyed druggies on't stairs getting out their heads and rowing. Screeching and shouting at each other like mad birds off an horror film. Honestly, come and see it. Come to my flat. Go on, you gotta come to my flat – you can buy it.

AJ*'s phone starts ringing.* TIA *reaches for the phone and picks it up.*

Is that the TV people?

AJ *snatches the phone from her hand and the ringing stops.*

AJ. Fuck you doing taking my phone? Take the piss, man. You don't go grabbing someone else's things. You cancelled the call you idiot.

Pause.

That was an important call. I needed to take that. Fuck's sake.

Pause.

TIA. Not nice shouting at people.

AJ. Don't take people's stuff then.

TIA. Always getting shouted at. You're not the secret millionaire.

AJ. I know! That's what I was trying to say.

TIA. A millionaire'd never treat someone like that.

Pause.

AJ. Look, I'm sorry. Okay?

TIA. Leave me alone.

AJ. I'm sorry I shouted. It was an important call and you had hold of it and
I just got… I'm sorry. I'm an idiot. I'm sorry. Let me make it up to you. How can I make it up to / you?

TIA. Gimme a fag.

AJ. I don't smoke.

TIA. Yes you do. I could smell it mixed in with your aftershave. Dolce and Gabbana.

AJ. You don't miss a trick you, do you.

AJ *takes a gold cigarette case from his jacket.*

TIA. Smooth.

AJ. Solid gold. Got my name inscribed in it. Look.

TIA. Is that in case you forget what yer called?

AJ. It was a present.

TIA. Who from?

AJ. A very good friend.

TIA. They must like you.

AJ. Yeah. I'd done him a few favours so
He's got his own modelling agency. Does proper
successfully you know.
In fact, I gotta tell ya, he'd be interested in you.

TIA. Shut up.

AJ. He would. Have you ever thought about doing modelling?

TIA. No.

AJ. You should. You're really pretty you know.

TIA. I'm not. I'm ugly.

AJ. No you're not! I swear. Look, I really shouldn't be giving a
girl your age cigarettes…

TIA. I have smoked for over two years.

AJ. How old are you?

TIA. Old enough.

AJ. Go on. How old?

TIA. Sixteen.

AJ. Don't lie. It doesn't make any difference to me.

TIA. I'm not lying.

AJ. I can tell. I'll give you a fag if you tell me how old you are.
Truthfully.

TIA. Nearly fifteen. You'd better still give me one now.

AJ. I will. Look, do you want me to put in a good word with my friend? He's always looking for new models. Especially your age. Let me take your photo. I'll show him and see what he says.

AJ *takes a photo of* TIA *with his phone*.

TIA. Let me see. (*Beat*.) Delete.

AJ. Do you not want me to see what he says?

AJ *takes another photo*.

TIA. You'd better delete them or I'm gettin the police.

AJ *takes a series of photos of* TIA.

AJ. Come on. You look amazing. Strike the pose. Look at that. / That's good.

TIA. Stop it!

AJ. Alright. Here.

AJ *hands her the cigarette case*. TIA *looks inside it*.

TIA. Why are they so skinny?

AJ. They're designer. If it's not designer, I don't wanna know ya.

TIA. How many can I have?

AJ. How many's in there?

TIA. Twelve.

AJ. Twelve then.

TIA. All of em?

AJ. Yeah.

TIA *takes the cigarettes out of the case*.

What you doin?

TIA. I thought…

AJ. Keep them in there.

TIA. But you said I / could.

AJ. You can have that as well.

TIA. Honestly?

AJ. Have it. Keep it. You like it don't you?

TIA. Yeah but I thought it was a present.

AJ. And now it's my present to you.

TIA. It's got your name on it.

AJ. So you'll always remember who gave it to you.

TIA. Sure?

AJ. It's yours.

TIA. That's well mint of yer.

AJ. And don't be going down Cash Generator and selling it for next to nothing.

TIA. I won't.

AJ. They'll rip you off anyway.

TIA. I love it. Thank you.

AJ. So am I forgiven?

TIA. Maybe.

AJ. Maybe?

TIA. Not much point me havin all these fags if I an't got me own lighter…

AJ. Push it don't ya. (*Beat*.) Here.

> AJ *takes a gold-plated lighter out of his jacket pocket and hands it to* TIA. *She goes to the doorway to smoke*.

What about your mate on the phone, what happened there?

TIA (*smoking*). Forget it.

AJ. Boyfriend?

TIA. No!

AJ. How you getting back to Freehold?

TIA. Got legs.

AJ. That's not a good idea, is it.

TIA. Why not?

AJ. Why'd you think?

TIA. I can look after myself.

AJ. It's the middle of winter and you're dressed like you're off down Ayia Napa. Why've you not got a proper coat on?

TIA. An't got one.

> AJ *takes a car key out of his pocket and places it on the table.*

> TIA *flicks away her fag and returns to the table. She stands close to* AJ.

> You've got a Mercedes?

AJ. Sure have.

TIA. And you don't get paid much?

AJ. I'm a good saver.

TIA. I like Mercedes.

AJ. I got an S-Class. Quality wheels, I tell you. When I was your age I said I would get a top car. Not messing about with no poor man's car. You should see it when I'm pulling up outside the club or the party, all the mouths wide open. Sometimes, yeah, I take the kids I work with, the older ones, I take them out into town. When they're with me, they can get in anywhere. They love it. Makes them feel proper special.

TIA. That's so nice of you to do that.

AJ. You got to help people where you can. Especially kids who've got hard lives and that. I prefer hanging round with younger people anyway. Can have more of a laugh than with people my age. Take you. You've told bare jokes tonight. You've made me laugh more tonight than Mushy has his whole life.

TIA. That's not hard.

AJ. I'm shootin off soon.
    If you want I could… I mean, if you wanted and –

TIA. What?

AJ. I could drop you home.

TIA. I'm not showing you where I live!

AJ. You wanted to give me the grand tour before!

TIA. You can drop me on the corner of Manchester Road,
    where the cash and carry is.

AJ. Unless that is, you wanna join this little mash-up I'm going
    to. Car's just outside.

TIA. Right…

AJ. So?
    Come with us if you want.

TIA. You'd let me in that car?

AJ. Yeah. If you're not –
    You could if you wanted.

TIA. Why would yer wanna do that?

AJ. I told you. You're a joker, init.

TIA. Whose party is it?

AJ. Good friends. They'd love you, you know.

3.

August, 2014.

A box room with a single bed in a flat above an off-licence. The off-licence is situated on a small precinct of shops and throughout the scene we should hear the occasional sounds of a few noisy passers-by, the melody of an ice-cream van and the odd siren disappearing elsewhere.

TIA, with blood on her clothes, frantically hammers on the bedroom door. Men with raised voices cause a commotion outside the room.

TIA. Swear to god I'm gunna kill him! Let me out of here!

More hammering on the door.

Open the door now! I tell yer what it is, yer'd better let me out of here or I swear to god…!

A car screeches round the corner outside and pulls up outside, its door opened and slammed shut almost immediately.

You're all a bunch of soft-arses! Scared of a girl!

More hammering on the door.

Let me out I'm gunna rip his head off!

TIA hurries to the window and tries to open it.

If I can't get out the door I'll climb out the window. Don't care how high it is.

TIA can't get the window open.

Oh well done, you've locked the windows as well! You bunch of fuckin –

TIA hurries back to the door and hammers on it again.

Let me out!

AJ (*from the other side of the door, out of breath*). Tia? It's me, it's AJ.

TIA. Let me out of here!

AJ. Tia, it's me, I'm back. I need you to calm down.

TIA. I don't give a toss what you need.

AJ. Just calm down.

TIA. I needed *you* but where were yer?

AJ. I'm coming in okay? Easy, yeah?

TIA. Swear to yer, as soon as you open that door I'm out of here and I'm gunna smash his face in. I'm gunna –

AJ. Who Tia? What's happened?

TIA. You know who. Graham. I'm gunna kill him!

AJ. Just calm down. I'm coming in, okay?

The door is unlocked and opened. As AJ *enters the room,* TIA *tries to get past him but he holds on to her.*

TIA. Get off me!

AJ. Calm down!

TIA. Let. Go. Of. Me!

AJ. Easy Tia, you're bleeding –

TIA. Get your hands off me!

They struggle and AJ *overpowers* TIA. *She shrieks as he throws her onto the bed.*

AJ. Tia, just stop!

They both catch their breath.

That's it. Easy, yeah? I'm just gonna lock this door and then I'm gonna make sure you're okay, yeah?

AJ *walks to the door and locks it.*

The blood Tia. Where's it from?

TIA. You left me on my own!

AJ. Are you alright?

TIA. Left me on my own with them – with *him*! I said last time I din't want him near me and you said okay and now yer've gone back on another / promise and –

AJ. I know. I'm sorry. I shouldn't have let him. I'm sorry. Come here, let me check you.

TIA. Don't touch me.

AJ. Tia there's blood –

TIA. What do you care?

AJ. Course I care. Where you cut?

TIA. Left me on my own with all them. Didn't even tell me you were going.

AJ. I didn't wanna interrupt –

TIA. Interrupt?!

AJ. I was only gonna be a minute. The traffic, it was –

TIA. Where were yer?

AJ. Don't worry. Where's the blood coming from?

TIA. With yer fat-bitch wife? Playing mummies and daddies were yer? I hope she loses that baby, the –

AJ slaps TIA's face.

Short silence.

AJ. Take that back.

TIA. You're worse than them.

AJ. Take it back.

TIA. Why should I?

AJ. It's horrible. It's a disgusting thing to say.

TIA. You wanna know what's disgusting? Having Graham, that nasty, stinking pig on top of yer. Having his sweat drippin all over yer. You said you wun't let him near me ever again!

AJ. I wouldn't have if I was –

TIA. He were digging his big girly nails into me, tearing at ma skin, right into the flesh, and he were doin it on purpose – ripping into ma sides and into ma back… I tried to stop him but I couldn't move my arms, I were too hammered. He kept wiping blood on my top and laughing, and I remember thinking that it's my new top that you got me from Top Shop and how you'd get angry when you saw't state of it.

AJ. Don't worry about that. We'll get you some new tops.

TIA. I were screaming for him to get off me but he just kept on doing it and laughing at me.

AJ. So you smashed a bottle in his eye.

TIA. Can't remember.

AJ. You definitely did. He's had to go A&E.

TIA. Good.

AJ. It's not good.

TIA. It's me who needs to go A&E. I told you not to let him come near me ever again.

AJ. What am I supposed to do? I didn't know he was gonna come.

TIA. Yes you did because he's paid yer. He told me. How much has he give yer? Am I gunna see any of it? Thought not.

AJ. What you on about?

TIA. Don't lie to me AJ! He said it himself! You knew he were coming so don't lie.

    A beat.

AJ. It was out of my hands. I couldn't do nowt about it.

TIA. You promised me.

AJ. I did try but they wouldn't take no for an answer.

TIA. Since when do they tell you what to do?

AJ. Not them. Pin. He said.

TIA. Pin? What's it gotta do with Pin?

AJ. Forget it.

TIA. What's it gotta do with Pin? AJ?

AJ. He's involved now.

TIA. *Involved?* What's that supposed to mean?

AJ. It means what it means.

TIA. Why've you done that? AJ? Why've you done that?

AJ. What am I gonna say? No?

TIA. Yes!

AJ. Not to him.

TIA. He scares me AJ. He's not right in the head.

AJ. Exactly. So how'm I meant to say no to him?

TIA. What if he comes here? What if he... –

AJ. Yeah well he might come now that you've bottled his best mate.

TIA. Why've you done that? AJ?

AJ. I owe him money.

TIA. What's that gotta do with it?

AJ. That's it. That's why.

TIA. So why should... No. You haven't.

AJ. What?

TIA. How could you do that you –

TIA *starts hitting* AJ.

How could you?

AJ. What you doin?

TIA. Using me to...

AJ. Get off!

TIA. Using me to pay your debts you... –

AJ. Quit it you stupid cow!

TIA. I trusted you!

AJ. Stop!

    AJ *grabs hold of her.*

    Stop.

TIA. You've ruined everything.

    TIA *gives up trying to hit him.*

    I trusted you.

AJ. It'll be alright, I promise. I'll make sure of it.

TIA. You're not in charge no more.

AJ. Course I am. Who do you think they phoned when you started going crazy? I swear to ya, as soon as they called me, I got in the car straight away. I put my toe down Tia. Honestly. But the traffic was just mental, I swear. Bumper to bumper all the way back to your old school. Listen Tia, all I could think about was you. There was all these girls playing netball out on the playground –

TIA. Eyeing up fresh meat?

AJ. No. They looked about your age. Had those coloured bibs with the letters, and the little skirts. I watched them jumping up and down in front of each other, arms waving like little stars. Like their lives depended on it. And I thought, what a shame. All them girls being forced to do that; to care about a pointless ball going in a net – and there's my Tia making something of herself. It's bare hot in here you know. Need some air.

    AJ *walks to the window and takes out keys. He opens the curtains, unlocks the window and opens it.*

    Weather like this people just go crazy. Can't handle the heat. Can't handle their tempers. (*Beat.*) Why don't you sit down? Come on. Sit on the bed here.

TIA. Don't wanna.

AJ. Come on. You need to rest. Just sit down so we can chat properly like we used to do.

    TIA *sits down.*

That's better. Move up.

AJ *sits next to her.*

Wanna smoke?

AJ *lights a cigarette and gives it to* TIA.

Here.

AJ *lights a cigarette for himself.*

Remember when we first got together and I'd ring you every night before you went bed?

TIA. You used to be so nice to me.

AJ. Still am nice to you. We used to have proper chats back then.

TIA. Never knew a man could spend so long on't phone. You were like an old woman.

AJ. Thanks.

TIA. You can still do it you know. Ring me an that. If you want to.

AJ. I do want to.

TIA. You can then. Have our night-time chats. Making plans. Do you remember all the plans?

AJ. Of course I do. Our plans for world / domination.

TIA. World domination.

AJ. Us / against the world.

TIA. Against the world.

AJ. We'll take them all / on.

TIA. And we'll take them down.

AJ. That's the one.

TIA. Yeah, it'd be good, if you wanted to, y'know, ring me an that.

AJ. Yeah it would. I will. Can't every night though. I have got –

TIA. No, I know. I'm not saying –

AJ. Because I got a lot on right now.

TIA. I know.

AJ. More than I used to so –

TIA. A couple of times a week maybe.

AJ. I'm sure we'll be able to sort something.

TIA. And maybe we could go away somewhere. Like we said we would.

AJ. We'll see, yeah?

TIA. D'yer remember? We said we'd get in the car and get out of here.

AJ (*reading a text on his phone*). Did we?

TIA. It were your idea!

AJ. Was it?

TIA. You said we should go and see some new places.

AJ. Oh yeah, I do remember something.

TIA. That'd be so nice. I'd love it if we could do that. Can we do that?

AJ. We'll see.

TIA. I don't even care where we go, just so long as it's an hotel somewhere with a big bed and clean sheets. And one of those baths, the ones in the chocolate adverts. I'd run you a bubble bath and you'd get in and I'd wash your hair really nice like they do in't hairdressers and I'd scrub your back and that. And then I could get in and get clean and you could shave me just how you –

AJ *stands*.

AJ. As if I've got time for a holiday.

TIA. I just meant –

AJ. You say some dumb things you know. How am I going to go on holiday with you? What am I going to say to my pregnant wife? Didn't think of that did yer. I can't just – Oh don't start

What you crying for? Don't cry. What's up with you? Oh come on, I'm just all wound up. This Pin stuff. And Graham. It's got me properly stressed out right now. I do care about you and I do want to go away with you. You're my number-one girl.

Pause.

TIA. Not your number-one girl.

AJ. What you on about? Course you are –

TIA. Who were you with before?

AJ. I told you –

TIA. And don't lie because I can smell some cheap Britney Spears spray all over you. It's clingin to the back of my throat.

AJ. What you on about? It's probably yours.

TIA. I wun't wear that nastiness. Who were you with?

AJ. No one. Honestly.

TIA. Don't lie! All what I do for you and you go running off with some / other slag.

AJ. It's not like that. I was –

TIA. After all I've done for you.

AJ. All you've done for me? Are you kidding me? What about all the stuff I do for you?

TIA. What do you do for me?

AJ. Who topped up your phone? Who buys you fags? Who buys you booze? Eh? Come on. Who got you that top? You're getting expensive Tia.

TIA. I never asked for any of it.

AJ. You always take it though.

TIA. Yeah but –

AJ. Take, take, take. That's you. And never give nowt back.

TIA. What do you mean, never give nowt back? That's –

AJ. You never buy me anything.

TIA. With what money?

AJ. Exactly. It's not an equal relationship.

TIA. How'm a supposed to buy you some't when I don't have no money?

AJ. I give you money.

TIA. You said you was gonna give me twenty quid an yer never did.

AJ. Who did?

TIA. You did. Before we got to Mo's. You said –

AJ. Supposed to be doing me a favour. Friends charge each other to do favours now do they?

TIA. Friends? Is that what I am?

AJ. I swear if it keeps happening we might have to knock this on the head.

TIA. What yer saying AJ?
I know you do a lot for me.

AJ. Damn right I do. I never get nothing back in return.

TIA. Just tell me what you want and I'll do it.

AJ. Forget it. You can't give me anything I want.

TIA. Please, tell me. What do you want me to do?

Pause.

AJ. They're proper into you, them lot out there. You got a following. And the thing is, they know that when I make a promise I stick to it. You know what I'm saying?

TIA. Please don't AJ.

AJ. I think you're gonna need a little bit more vodka. Don't you? I got another bottle here.

TIA. Not now. Please AJ. Don't let them –

AJ. Can't go back on a promise.

TIA *starts to cry.*

TIA. Please. I hurt really bad. Everywhere hurts really bad.

AJ. It won't once you've had some of this.

TIA. Please. I'll do anything you want if we can go now.
Anything. And I won't ask for owt and I won't even –

AJ. There's no point going round in circles. It's happening. Are
you having some of this or not? I said, are you having some
of this or not?

TIA. I'm goin straight to police when I get out of here.

AJ *laughs*.

AJ. Do you think I'm scared? What are they gonna do?

TIA. Arrest you.

AJ. Like last time? You know the score. It'll be you who gets
banged up for whorin yourself out.

TIA. I'll tell em what Graham done. I'll show em.

AJ. Do it! He's white, they'll arrest him. Think they're gonna
touch me? Too scared to arrest a Paki.

TIA. Not when I tell em what you done.

AJ. You know what? Forget it. You can go. I don't care any
more. You been doing my head in for time now so we might
as well call it a day. I got plenty of other girls lined up.
Plenty. Much prettier than you an all. So go on. Get out.

TIA. Why are you so horrible to me?

AJ. Look at the state of you. I'm gonna have to let them all
down now, tell them the party's cancelled. Do you know how
that's gonna make me look? But I don't care. It'll be worth it
to finally get rid of you.

Pause.

TIA. Let them in then.

AJ. Nah, too late for that now.

TIA. I'm sorry. AJ. Please. Let them in.

AJ. You're just gonna embarrass me again, I know it.

TIA. I won't, I promise. I'll get myself cleaned up and ready and it'll be fine and you won't have to cancel and it'll all be okay. Please!

AJ picks up the unopened vodka bottle.

AJ. Drink then.

AJ forces vodka into TIA's mouth, we hear it glug as he holds it in place. He removes the bottle and TIA coughs and retches.

TIA. More.

AJ. More?

TIA snatches the bottle from AJ and swigs.

TIA. Get them then.

AJ. Clean yourself up.

AJ moves to the door and exits, locking the door afterwards.

TIA hurries to the window and climbs onto the windowsill.

TIA (*to herself, as she struggles to haul herself up*). Don't care how high it is. Anything's better'n this. Anything.

TIA climbs out of the window and hangs from the frame outside.

Let go Tia. You need to let go.

A key starts to unlock the door.

Now!

TIA drops out of the window and drops down into the street below. Screams from witnesses as TIA's body thuds onto the pavement below.

4.

August, 2014.

A specialist video-interview suite at Bootle Street Police Station, Manchester.

Two sofas, a table, a video camera on a tripod, and a CCTV camera.

SIMON *is pushing* TIA, *who is in a wheelchair, into the interview suite.* TIA *has both legs in plaster, bandages on both forearms and is wearing a neck brace.*

SIMON (*struggling with the pushing*). This from a museum? Like a bleedin antique.

TIA. I can do it meself.

SIMON. Weighs a ton.

TIA. I said I can do it meself.

SIMON. Only tryna help.

> SIMON *adjusts a video camera as* TIA *wheels herself in front of it.*

I've just gotta get this in the right place.
Shouldn't be a sec.
(*Struggling with the camera.*) How'd yer…?
Can't bloody…
Sorry about this Tia. Won't be a sec.
(*Into radio.*) Someone were supposed to've done this already
Must be this thing here
There we are.

> SIMON *sits down on the sofa and then immediately jumps up again. He hurries to the camera and presses record.*

Nearly forgot to press record!
Right, we'll make a start then.
Conducting this interview is Detective Inspector Sladden, overseeing is Detective Inspector Sallis. The time is eleven fourteen on August the twenty-seventh, twenty fourteen.
Right then, Tia
If you could just…

State your full name for me, and date of birth, that would be…
Okay?

TIA. Tia-Mae Ratt–

SIMON. Hold on.
Can you just –
Should've said –
You'll have to speak a bit louder than that.

TIA. My name is Tia-Mae Rattigan and my date of birth is the
sixteenth of July, nineteen-ninety-nine.

SIMON. Definitely loud enough. Thanks Tia. Right then…

SIMON *sits down on a sofa and opens an A4 notebook on
his lap.*

So…
Cancer. Right?

TIA.…

SIMON. You're cancer, aren't yer?
Sixteenth of July.
Your star sign.
It is isn't it?

TIA *shrugs.*

Do you not know?
I thought you were all –
Are yer not into all that? No?
Yer not bothered?
Nah. Load of rubbish anyway. Yer right to ignore it.
Right.

Look at yer. My word. Got yerself into a bit of a pickle
haven't yer. Ey?

TIA.…

SIMON. Got yerself into a right pickle I'd say. Flippin heck.
Last time you decide to jump out of a window, ey? Won't be
doing that again in an hurry will yer?
Right then, let's get started. Why don't you tell me what
happened.

TIA….

SIMON. You are happy to proceed with this interview aren't
    you, Tia?
    Because if you're not –

TIA. Yeah, I –

SIMON. Because if you're not
    If you're not happy to proceed…

TIA. I am, I –

SIMON. If you're not going to –
    There's not a lot of –

TIA. I am!

SIMON. Good.
    So why don't you tell me what happened then.
    Nice and clear.

TIA. Erm
    What, from –
    I'm not sure what…

SIMON. Tell yer what
    I'll tell yer what I'll do
    I'll ask a few questions, you tell me the answers and then
    we'll call it a day. Alright? Because it's been a bit of a
    stinker today so I'd appreciate it if you just answered my
    questions. Alright?
    Is that alright Tia? Yeah? (*Looks at notebook.*) So…
    You were at the home of Mushtaq Iqbal on Thursday the
    fourteenth of August. Is that correct?

TIA. Thursday the
    I'm, erm –
    Don't know when it were.

SIMON. I'm talking about when you –
    When you did that to yourself. Had your accident. You were
    at Mushtaq Iqbal's house in Deeplish. Is that correct?

TIA. Yeah. I were at Mushy's. We call him Mushy.

SIMON. Okay, let's call him Mushy. So you were at Mushy's
    house and what was it you were doing round there?

TIA. What were we doin?

SIMON. Yeah. What were you doing round at Mushy's?

TIA. Just
    Chillin.

SIMON. Chilling?

TIA. Yeah.

SIMON. And when you say chilling, what exactly do you mean
    by that?

TIA. Just –
    (*Shrugs.*)

SIMON. What exactly does it mean? What is it that you're
    actually doing when you're chilling?

TIA. Just
    Sat round.
    Having a laugh an that.

SIMON. So you're sat round at Mr Iqbal's house and you're
    having a laugh. Have I got that right so far?

TIA. Yeah.

SIMON. And who else was there that afternoon?

TIA. There were a load.

SIMON. Who Tia?

TIA. I try to picture em all but
    It's like
    I can't.

SIMON. So you're not going to tell us who was there? Is that
    correct?

TIA. It's not that, it's
    I know it's there somewhere
    I know I know who was there
    But
    My brain won't let me remember. It's all
    Like, foggy.

SIMON. Had you been drinking that day Tia?

TIA. It's not that
That's not why I can't remember.

SIMON. So you had been drinking?

TIA. Yeah. But not so that I couldn't –

SIMON. And how much had you drunk that day?

TIA. A bit.

SIMON. How much is a bit?

TIA *shrugs*.

Come on Tia. This is important. How much had you had to drink?

TIA. I don't know.
Some vodka and some
I don't remember properly.

SIMON. That's what drink does. Dun't mix too well with being a reliable witness.

TIA. What d'yer mean?

SIMON. Is there anyone you can remember being there?

TIA. Graham. He were there.

SIMON. Yep. So Graham Wild, we know about him.

TIA. Yeah, he were the one that –

SIMON. You know he ended up in hospital don't you?

TIA. So did I.

SIMON. Bottle to the face. He's pressing charges –

TIA. No, that's not –

SIMON. Says you rammed a bottle in his face because he caught you stealing from him.

TIA. No I did not –

SIMON. His right eye was almost detached from his face.

TIA. Good! I'd do it again if I saw him the fat fuckin piece of –

SIMON. Enough of that. When you're being interviewed by me, you mind your language. Not having talk like that in here.

TIA. If you knew what he done then you'd be arrestin him / and –

SIMON. Just hold it there. At this stage I only want to know who was there. We can talk about what happened later. So Graham Wild was there. Who else?

TIA. You'd better arrest him.

SIMON. We can talk about that later. Just tell me who was there.

TIA. Mushy. He were there.

SIMON. Yeah I'd assumed that. Who else?

TIA. I, I –

SIMON. How many people do you think were there?

TIA. I don't know
   Eight?
   Ten maybe.

SIMON. How many of them can you remember?

TIA. Graham, Mushy
   Viral I think.

SIMON. Viral?

TIA. Yeah.

SIMON. I presume that's not his real name?

TIA. Don't know his real name
   That's what everyone calls him
   Drives a taxi.

SIMON. Do you know what taxi company he works for?

TIA. Radio Cars.

SIMON. Right. Anyone else?

TIA. Kaz
I don't know his proper name either.

SIMON. Is there anything else you know about this Kaz
character?

TIA. He's old.

SIMON. How old?

TIA. Well old. Like…
Forty or some't.

SIMON. Do you know what he does for a living?

TIA. No.

SIMON. Anyone else?

TIA.…

SIMON. Who Tia? Who else was there?

TIA *looks at* SIMON.

Was there someone else?

TIA. Who've yer spoke to?

SIMON. I'm asking you Tia, who was –

TIA. If you've already spoke to em, what's the point? Why'm I
gunna tell you who was there when you already know?

SIMON. It's important we hear from you as well.

TIA. So you already know who was there?

SIMON. We've spoken to a number of individuals and we've
got a pretty good idea who was there but I really want to
hear it from you. Who else was there? You have to say.

TIA. You already know so –

SIMON. Yeah so it won't matter if you tell us will it. Won't
make any difference. No one'll know what you've said Tia.

TIA. How do you know?

SIMON. Because it's my job to make sure of it.

TIA. That's not what happened last time.

SIMON. I don't know about that.

TIA. You told him that I'd grassed! I came to yer and told yer what'd been happenin and you went to him and told him that I'd grassed!

SIMON. I'm not aware / of –

TIA. Got my fuckin head kicked in for that.

SIMON. Tia, I've told you about / your language.

TIA. So why should I believe you now?

SIMON. Because I was nothing to do with it.

TIA. You're all the same.

SIMON. Tia, listen to me now. Whatever happened in the past, forget about it. I promise you, only the police involved in the case will find out about what you've said today. Okay?

TIA. You can't speak for all t'rest of em. You don't know what they'll do.

SIMON. Trust me Tia. No one's going to put you in danger. Remember what I said: we've heard from the others already so you telling us a few names won't make any difference as far as they're concerned. They've all grassed each other up anyway.
Who else was there?

Tia, who else was there?

TIA. AJ.

SIMON. AJ?

TIA. Yeah.

SIMON. Do you know his full name?

TIA *looks at* SIMON.

Can you tell me please Tia.

TIA. Anjam Akhtar.

SIMON. Anjam Akhtar.

TIA *nods*.

Right.

TIA. What yer gunna do now?

SIMON. Were there any other girls there?

TIA. Why?

SIMON. Answer the question.

TIA. I were the only girl.

SIMON. No one else your own age?

TIA. Why'd yer wanna know?

SIMON. Just answer me Tia. Was there anyone else your age?

TIA. No.

Short pause.

SIMON. What were you thinking? Jesus Christ, Tia. What's a girl your age doing hanging round with grown men?

Pause.

Sorry but
I can't get my head around it
What were you doing?

TIA. I don't know.

SIMON. No offence, but why would grown men want to hang around with a fourteen-year-old girl?

TIA *shrugs*.

Can you see it from my point of view, Tia? It doesn't make any sense, does it. Help me out here. Why on earth would grown men want to hang around a fourteen-year-old girl? What's in it for them?

TIA. What do you think!

SIMON. What do *I* think? It's not my place to say. That's why I'm asking you.

TIA. Yer doin my head in now.

SIMON. Okay. Different question. What's in it for you?

TIA. What d'yer mean?

SIMON. Why do you hang about with them?

TIA. Cos…

SIMON. Do they give you money?

TIA.…

SIMON. Tia. Are you –
    If you're taking money off them to –
    You know –
    If they're paying you –
    Are they paying you, Tia?
    Because if they are, there's nothing we can do you know.

TIA. They're my mates!

SIMON. They're your mates.
    Do you think it's normal for a fourteen-year-old girl to be
    mates with forty-year-old men?

TIA. How should I know?

SIMON. Tia, I don't think you understand how serious this is.
    We've got you and all your injuries. We've got a teenage girl
    in a house with a load of men. We've got a man almost
    blinded who's accusing you of Grievous Bodily Harm as
    well as attempted theft –

TIA. I didn't nick owt from him!

SIMON. We've got all this and you're not telling me anything.

TIA. I did not nick owt from that lying –

SIMON. So as it stands, all I can do is arrest you for assaulting
    Mr Wild.

TIA. You can't arrest me, I was –

SIMON. Based on what we've been told, Tia, that's all we
    can do.

TIA. You can't believe *him*!

SIMON. Why wouldn't we? Far as I can see, he's an hard-
    working man, never been in trouble with the police.

TIA. No
    No
    That's wrong, you can't –

SIMON. There's no reason not to believe him.

TIA. You can't
    You can't blame me
    Not after what he did to me
    It's not me who –
    How comes I'm always the one gettin in shit? How comes he
    just gets away with it?

SIMON. Gets away with what, Tia? What / did he do?

TIA. You don't know what you're doing
    You don't have a clue what you're doing.
    Fuck this. You don't know what he done to me.

SIMON. So tell me then! How can I know anything if you don't
    bleedin tell me!
    Do you see what I'm saying? You're not telling me anything.

    Tia, what did he do?

TIA. He…

SIMON. Please Tia. Tell me. Did Graham Wild do something
    to you?

    TIA *nods*.

    Okay. What did he do?

TIA. He…

    SIMON *offers* TIA *a tissue. She takes one.*

SIMON. Come on. What did he do?

TIA. He…
    Did stuff to me, he…

    Short pause.

SIMON. Okay. I need you to tell us what it was that he did to
    you.

TIA. He... –

SIMON. And Tia. I need you to think very carefully about what you're going to say now, right?
What did Graham Wild do to you?

TIA. He ripped my clothes.

SIMON. He ripped your clothes?

TIA. Yeah. He ripped my clothes and he like scratched me with his –
He's got these long nails, and he dug em in me and cut me all down my sides here – (*Indicates where she was injured.*) and all over my back.

SIMON. So he scratched you with his nails. Is that correct?

TIA. And he ripped my clothes.

SIMON. Okay he scratched you and he ripped your clothes. I'll make a note of that for the –

TIA. And then he pulled my jeans down and he...

Pause.

He pulled my jeans down, he got on top of me and he...

SIMON *offers* TIA *another tissue.*

SIMON. What did he do after that?

TIA. He...
He did it to me.

SIMON. Did what?

TIA. You know what I'm saying.

SIMON. I think I do, yes Tia. But I need you to say it. What did he do?

TIA. I didn't want him near me, he's disgusting, I tried to stop him and I –

SIMON. Please can you tell me what he did.

TIA. What d'yer think! He made me have sex with him.

FOUR

SIMON. Tia, this is a serious allegation. You understand that, right?

TIA. He wouldn't get off me and he were hurting me really bad –

SIMON. So Graham Wild raped you?

TIA. Yes!

SIMON. Was anyone else in the flat at the time?

TIA. They were all watchin and laughin and getting their phones out.

SIMON. Okay. Let me just
Right
You didn't say anything at the time did you?

TIA. I don't know what I said.

SIMON. You didn't. Why didn't you? Why didn't you report it at the time?

TIA. I,
I don't know, I –

SIMON. Okay.
This is a very serious allegation. And just so we're absolutely clear – you're not saying this because you think it'll get you out of trouble are you?

TIA. I'm tellin the truth!

SIMON. Alright. What we're going to do is
We'll take a little break. I'm going to speak to a few people and we'll get you checked out.

TIA. You don't believe me.

SIMON. It's not a matter of whether I believe you or not. We've got to investigate haven't we. And then it's up to others whether they believe you.

TIA. But you don't though. I can tell.

SIMON. Actually, Tia, I do. I do believe you. And we're going to make sure you're alright from now. Okay? (*Wrapping things up.*) So we'll just call it a / day for now and then –

ow yer gunna do that? How yer gunna make sure I'm
ght?

N. Don't worry Tia, we know what we're doing. Okay?

Pause.

TIA. How comes yer need two cameras?

SIMON. Say again.

TIA. What d'yer need two cameras for?

Are they checkin you're doing your job properly?

Blackout.

5.

October, 2014.

A bridge over a small river on the edge of town. Clouding over.

TIA, *curled up in a ball on the floor, puts her phone in her pocket and then tries to drag herself to the champagne bottle but can't reach it.*

TIA. Yer've fucked it, yer've fucked it, yer've fucked it.

Come here you little…

She tries with all her might to reach the bottle but can't.

Bastard.

She takes out her phone and makes a call. No answer. She tries again. Leaves a voicemail:

Call me back. PLEASE.

TIA *puts her phone away and attempts once again to reach the bottle. She fails.*

TIA *reaches into the wheelchair and pulls out a half-litre bottle of vodka. She pours a shot into the lid and downs it.*

She pours another shot into the lid and downs that. And another. She then swigs from the bottle.

Yer all fuckin bastards.

TIA *puts the bottle down and tries to get the wheelchair the right way up. This is difficult for her and soon she is too exhausted to continue.*

Come on move you –
Come on
Move!

TIA *takes out her phone and makes another call. No answer. She tries again. Leaves a voicemail:*

Please ring me back. I need yer!

She puts the phone away.

TIA *tries to push the wheelchair with every bit of strength she has left.*

Will you just…
Yer so weak
Come on!
Just
Fuckin
Move!

She isn't able to move the wheelchair and in frustration starts hitting the arm rests and the wheels.

Useless piece of fuckin
Why'd yer have to be so…

(*Roars.*) IT'S NOT FUCKING FAIR.

TIA *puts her head in her hands and sobs.*

Not fucking fair.

KATIE *enters. She sees TIA and stops, watches her for a moment.*

KATIE. Dunno what you're crying for.

TIA. You came back.

KATIE. Only cos you've got my food.

TIA. You came back.

KATIE. Lucky ain't ya.

TIA. Katie, I'm –

KATIE. Don't wanna hear it. Just came for my food.

KATIE *walks towards* TIA.

TIA. Can't tell yer how happy I am yer came back.

KATIE. So you can take the piss outta me some more?

TIA. No. Katie, I –

KATIE. You really upset me and I thought we were supposed /
to be…

TIA. I'm such a horrible person. I'm…

KATIE *picks up the champagne bottle*.

KATIE. Bit of a waste, wasn't it.

TIA. Hair needed a wash anyway.

KATIE. There's a little bit left if…

TIA. Wet enough, ta.

You have it.

KATIE *downs the remaining champagne. She places the
bottle on the ground*.

Katie, I'm sorry
Not nice to take the piss like that.

KATIE. No.

TIA. Won't do it again. Promise.

KATIE. Or I'll leave you down here for good.

TIA *raises her arms for a hug*.

TIA. Is it alright if…

KATIE. Go on then.

KATIE *turns the wheelchair the right way up. She then hugs* TIA, *lifting her back into the wheelchair.*

TIA. 'S what best mates do in't it. Know how to wind each other up. Just shows we're close dun't it.

KATIE. Do you mean that? Best mates?

TIA. Course I do.

KATIE. Lucky we met each other ain't we?

TIA. Yeah.

KATIE. Now gimme my food, I've proper got the munchies.

TIA. Already?

KATIE. You know me, always thinking about food.

TIA *takes a plastic bag out of her bag. She removes a polystyrene box from the bag and hands it to* KATIE.

TIA. Think that's your one.

KATIE *opens the box.*

KATIE. Urggh what the hell's that?

TIA. Let's have a look.
That's mine.

KATIE. What are they? They look nasty.

TIA. Onion bhajis –
Never had one?

KATIE. Not ones that look like that. Eww.

TIA. They're well nice. Have one.

KATIE. That is proper nasty.

TIA. Thought you were into trying new things?

KATIE *takes an onion bhaji from the box and inspects it.*

Have a bite.

KATIE. If I get sick it's all your fault.

KATIE *takes a bite of the bhaji. She's impressed.*

TIA. See? I told yer.

KATIE. Not bad. Not bad at all.
How comes they give you free food? I'll be going back there
for sure.

TIA. Done em a few favours.

KATIE. What kind of favours?

TIA. Not like that.

KATIE. The one serving you
He kept
Well, maybe not, but
I thought he kept looking at me like… –

TIA. Like what?

KATIE. Nothing, just –

TIA. Think he fancies yer?

KATIE. No! I dunno
He did keep looking at me and smiling.

TIA. Maybe he does.
D'yer like him?

KATIE. Too old for me!

TIA. No he in't. Perfect age. Knows how to treat you right.
Has a bit of money. Not like the trampy little weasels back
at the Centre.

KATIE. Don't mention Centre. So glad we're not there right
now, sat in maths wanting to kill myself. Do you reckon
they'll call home?

TIA. I know they will.

KATIE. My mum's gonna KICK. OFF
What will your mum say?

TIA. She's not my mum.

    KATIE *laughs*

KATIE. You serious? But I thought –

TIA. I call her Mum cos it's easier but…

KATIE. What is she…?

TIA. Foster mum. Nadine. Fat bitch. She's happy as long as freezer's full of Mars ice creams. Not the proper ones, the little ones cos she says she's watching her obesity even though she canes the whole box before *Coronation Street*'s even got to the adverts.

KATIE. What about your real mum?

TIA. I been doin shots of voddy so you need to catch up.

TIA *takes out the vodka bottle and downs a shot. She passes the bottle to* KATIE.

KATIE *does a shot of vodka and passes the bottle back to* TIA.

Took me away from her when I were three. Not allowed to see each other no more cos Social Services are a bunch of thick fucking cunts that's why
I mean, I wanna be with her and she wants to be with me so what's the problem? They don't have a clue.

TIA *downs another shot of vodka and then passes the bottle to* KATIE.

An now I'm stuck with lazy-arse Nadine.

KATIE. What will she say if the Centre call her?

TIA. She dun't say owt no more. Given up after all the battles.

KATIE. Mine'll go ape-shit. Seriously.

KATIE *downs a shot of vodka.*

TIA. Tell her to fuck off.

KATIE. You ain't met my mum. Even she says she looks like Mike Tyson with tits. I'll just have to tell her it was your fault. You led me astray.

TIA. Led astray by a girl in a wheelchair. Takes some doin, that.

KATIE. I know, right? Led astray by a girl in a wheelchair and forced to drink stolen champagne in the countryside.

What has my life become? It's a tragedy! I may have to throw myself in this raging torrent of a river just to escape the brutality of it all.

TIA. Go on then.

KATIE. Thought you was gonna start being nice.

TIA. Jokin. (*Beat.*) They're having a party them lot.

KATIE. Who?

TIA. Them from t'kebab shop. An house party. They're always mint.

KATIE. Tia. What the hell? You've been to house parties at Mr Kebabshop's?

TIA. What's the big deal?

KATIE. They're old, for a start.

TIA. Told yer, they're perfect age for girls like us. So… Do you wanna go to it? It's tonight.

KATIE. No I don't think so.

TIA. Why not?

KATIE. I just don't think that –
    Probably won't –
    Don't really feel like it.

TIA. Are yer not allowed?

KATIE. Yeah

TIA. What time are you allowed out till?

KATIE. Whenever.

TIA. We could go just for a bit and you know, check it out.

KATIE. Nah. Next time maybe.

TIA. What's up? They're really nice you know. And they all have cars and'll drop you home at whatever time you need to be back for. They're really good like that. Come on. It'll be good!

KATIE. Dunno. I'd have to speak to my mum. And if the Centre have grassed me up she's definitely not going to let me.

TIA. Your mum wun't even find out. They'll come and get us from here.

KATIE. So I could just tell her that you needed to go somewhere and had no one else to help. She'll believe that.

TIA. What, she knows who I am?

KATIE. Yeah, course. I was telling her about you the other day.

TIA. Was yer?

KATIE. She was asking about how I was getting on at Centre and I said how much better it was since you got there. I was properly depressed at the end of Year 9 and she was getting a bit worried about me, so this was like a bit of a boost for her. Told her how I'm like your driver
But not really a driver cos it's you who's sat down
More of a pusher but that don't sound right –

TIA. The word yer after is slave.

KATIE. You reckon? Thing is, Tia, a slave don't have the freedom to leave. I do. So watch what you say or I might just do that.
Anyway, Mum asked if you –
I mean, I want you to an all –
But she asked –
If… –

TIA. What?

KATIE. Oh you probably won't want to so –
What am I doing? Ignore me.

TIA. What you on about?

KATIE. So you're probably gonna say no –
And that's fine cos I understand that it's not exactly –

TIA. What?

KATIE. So my mum asked –
She's such a –
She wondered if –
If you wanted to, like, come to ours for –
You know.
If you wanted to come over for dinner an that?

TIA. What, she wants me to…?
    What…? Are you askin me to…?

KATIE. It's alright if you can't, I mean –

TIA. No it's not that –

KATIE. It's fine if you can't.

TIA. So she'd cook and we'd…?

KATIE. And we'd eat, yeah. She cooks, we eat. That's how it
    works.

TIA. What, all eat together?

KATIE. Yeah I know, it's so embarrassing
    It's my mum, she's –
    Just say no, it's fine. I / understand.

TIA. Wait. So when you say dinner, do yer mean like… Dinner
    like dinnertime, like twelve o'clock an that or… –

KATIE. No, in the evening! To come over in the evening.

TIA. So you mean tea?

KATIE. Tea, dinner, whatever you wanna call it.

TIA. That's so…

KATIE. Blame my mum
    So embarrassing.

TIA. No I mean, it's so –
    I've never been –
    I mean, nobody's ever asked me before.

KATIE. I won't be offended if you don't want –

TIA. Yes! Please. Yes.

KATIE. You would?

TIA. Yes! Nobody's ever asked me round before. I, I –
    When?

KATIE. Whenever you want. My mum's a wicked cook. She's
    doing a lot of her Jamaican classics at the moment so be
    prepared for something spicy and smoky. Irie yu ras clart!

Are you sure you'll be alright getting there? Maybe my mum
can pick you up.
And if you want, I think it would –
Don't you think it'd be cool if you stayed the night too?
Like, a sleepover. We got a blow-up mattress.

TIA. I've never done a sleepover! I'd really really like that! I'll
be able to see what your room's like and all your photos and
meet your mum and…

KATIE. You okay?

TIA. Yeah.

KATIE. Are you crying?

TIA. Just pissed.

KATIE. Aw Tia, come here.

   KATIE *hugs* TIA.

   What you bein silly for? Ey?

TIA. I'm sorry.

   TIA *begins to sob*.

KATIE. Aw babe, what is it? It's okay. We'll go get some more
food and sober up a bit and then we'll go to the party. What
do you say to that? Good idea?

   TIA *grips* KATIE *tighter.*

TIA. I'm sorry. For everything.

KATIE. What for you daft cow?

TIA. I'm so sorry.

KATIE. Holding me a bit hard.

   KATIE *tries to move away but* TIA *holds tight*.

   It's actually hurting.
   Tia, can you just –

TIA. I'm the worst –

KATIE. Tia, what the hell? You're hurting me!

> KATIE *releases herself from* TIA*'s grip.*

> Why you being such a weirdo? What's wrong with you?

TIA. I'm so sorry Katie. I don't deserve you. I deserve to die.

KATIE. What's happened? Tia? I don't get it, what's –

TIA. Gimme that.

> TIA *snatches the vodka from* KATIE *and swigs from the bottle.*

> KATIE *tries to take the bottle from* TIA.

KATIE. Don't think you should have any more of that.

> TIA *lashes the bottle out of* KATIE*'s reach.*

TIA. I'll drink as much as I fucking like.

> TIA *swigs from the bottle.*

> I'm gunna tell yer some't, right. And then you're gunna walk away and leave me and –

KATIE. I'm not going to leave you –

TIA. You are, cos I'm tellin you.
    You have to.

KATIE. No, I'm not gonna –

TIA. Shut up. Right? Shut up and listen to me. It's important. If you don't listen to me, bad things're gunna happen.

KATIE. What bad things? What are you talking –

TIA. Shut up and listen. We an't got time for you to... –
    They're coming here now –

KATIE. Who?

TIA. Listen. You need to go because they're coming here. The men in the kebab shop, and some others that are even worse, they're coming here.

KATIE. I don't understand –

TIA. The party. The men. They're making me bring you so that –
I've told em we're here, you need to go.

KATIE. You're scaring me.

TIA. You should be scared. Go! Now!

KATIE. Tia, what the hell? I'm not leaving you

TIA (*indicating her legs*). See this. I didn't fall down steps.

KATIE. What are you talking about?

TIA. They did this to me.

KATIE. Who, the guys in the kebab shop?

TIA. Them and others.

KATIE. Tell me what happened.

TIA. And if you don't fucking go from here, right now, they're
gunna do it to you an all.

KATIE. Do what?

TIA. They make me do stuff. Force me to…
Sometimes two of em. Sometimes fucking ten of em, taking
it in turns.

KATIE. Oh my god, Tia. I'm right here to help you. Okay? You
hear me?

TIA. You don't understand. Look at me. Think anyone wants to
do owt with me any more? Course they don't. I'm damaged
goods.
I hate myself –
I said I'd… I told them about you.

Do you see what I'm saying?

KATIE *takes a sharp intake of breath*.

They needed a new girl to… And I said I'd help.

KATIE. How could you –

TIA. They know where we are so you need to get out of here.

KATIE. I don't know how you could do that to me.

TIA. That's who I am. Now fuck off.

TIA *finishes the vodka and throws the bottle.*

I'm not gunna say it again – go!

TIA *pushes herself in the wheelchair to the bank of the river. She tries to manoeuvre it so it will roll down the bank but the wheels get stuck. She slides out of the wheelchair onto the floor and drags herself towards the river.*

KATIE *runs over and stops her.*

Let go of me!

KATIE. If anyone's gonna push you in the river, it should be me.

TIA. Do it then!

KATIE. I should.

TIA. Go on!

KATIE. But you didn't do it Tia. You didn't do it. You told me.

TIA. They'll get you if you don't go. They made me think I were special and made me think I –
You see you, yeah? You've got these twinkling eyes, all bright and dancey. Always looking like they're up to somethin or working somethin out. Your whole face is kinda like that. Like things can go right when I'm with you. They will love taking that from you.

TIA*'s phone starts ringing.*

Fuck.

KATIE. Is it them?

The sound of a car's engine can be heard in the distance, getting closer.

TIA. You need to go. Run!

KATIE. I'm not leaving you.

TIA. I can hear a car. They're here! Fucking run!

KATIE. I'm not leaving you here. You're coming home with me.

KATIE *starts to push* TIA *in the wheelchair. It's a struggle.*

TIA. You'll never get me up that hill!

KATIE *stops the wheelchair suddenly and crouches at* TIA*'s feet.*

What yer doing?

KATIE. Get on my back. Get on my back now!

KATIE *helps* TIA *climb onto her back.* TIA *drops her mobile.*

TIA. My phone. I've dropped my phone!

KATIE. Forget it. Get your arms round me.

TIA. Let me get my phone.

KATIE. Hold on to me.

KATIE *wraps* TIA*'s arms around her and sets off moving with some difficulty.*

TIA. Yer not gunna be able to carry me up there. Just leave me here.

The car's engine stops and its doors can be heard slammed shut.

KATIE. I'm not leaving you.

TIA. Quick! I can see them!

KATIE. Ssshhhh. They haven't seen us. They're not going to get us. Trust me Tia.

KATIE *manages to quicken her steps and gradually they run up the hill together and exit.*

TIA*'s mobile rings.*

Blackout.

End.